SECOND GENERATION SCOTTISH DMUs

Colin J. Howat

AMBERLEY

First published 2020

Amberley Publishing
The Hill, Stroud
Gloucestershire, GL5 4EP

www.amberley-books.com

Copyright © Colin J. Howat, 2020

The right of Colin J. Howat to be identified as
the Author of this work has been asserted in
accordance with the Copyright, Designs and
Patents Act 1988.

ISBN 978 1 4456 9197 8 (print)
ISBN 978 1 4456 9198 5 (ebook)

British Library Cataloguing in Publication Data.
A catalogue record for this book is available from
the British Library.

Typesetting by Aura Technology and Software
Services, India. Printed in the UK.

Introduction

Love them or hate them, the development and introduction of the Pacer and Sprinter units in the UK was controversial. By the late 1970s it was well known that something had to be done to replace the mass of ageing first generation DMUs. No single design of new train would meet all the wants and needs of the different train operators and local government leaders. The British Railways Board (BRB) therefore went for two totally different designs of replacement DMU. First was a lightweight rail bus, which could be a single vehicle, or multiple coaches derived from road vehicle bus technology, mounted on a basic four-wheeled chassis, the other was a more conventional heavyweight DMU, from which the Class 15x Sprinters emerged.

The BRB, along with Leyland Buses of Workington, designed and commissioned a development vehicle, LEV1, which took to the main lines in the early 1980s. This vehicle was also tested and demonstrated in the USA with sights set on large export orders under the BR/Transmark banner. From the original development vehicle, other prototype cars were built forming two-car prototypes for use on the BR network, later classified as 140s. Looking more like a shed on wheels, this paved the way for the building of two- and three-car rail buses classified as 141, 142, 143 and 144. Due to low capacity issues, poor ride and bad performance, these units were not welcomed by most passengers and staff. In some cases, sets such as the West Country Class 142 'skipper' sets had to be withdrawn from service due to ride and squealing issues when working over heavily curved track. However, if it had not been for the development of these new sets many rural lines would have been lost. These sets provided a stop gap service until the development of future designs.

LEV1 had shown what was possible to achieve with just a single vehicle rail bus but, having fixed axles, there was only a maximum possible length for such a rail bus. To enable any new rail buses to replace the first generation DMUs, a design capable of taking more passengers was needed. On paper the principle was relatively straight forward: put two rail-mounted bus bodies back to back and connect them with a corridor connection and drawbar. A proposed two-car rail bus termed the Class 140 was not the replacement initially proposed by BR. Instead this role was intended to fall to the new Class 210 DEMUs with two Class 210 prototypes entering service in 1981. Large scale replacement of all first generation DMUs with new Class 210s appeared uneconomical and there was a large push by the Passenger Transport Executives (PTEs) to find a cheaper alternative. However, the PTEs were unwilling to pay for a replacement so a lightweight prototype was built. This came in the form of No. 140001 and was built at both BRELs Derby Litchurch Lane works and the Leyland works at Workington. Each vehicle was of the two-car formation and had an overall length of 53-ft 7-in. (16.35 m), a width of 8-ft (2.47 m) and a weight of 23 tonnes. The unit was fitted with two Leyland TL11 200 hp (149 kw) engines and had seating capacity for 102 passengers, with further space for 100 standing. Tightlock couplings were also fitted. The basic cab design was based on the production EMU Class 317s as it had trade union approval. Another odd feature fitted to No. 140001 was the power-operated pivoting double leaf swing plug doors that were based on a design used by Netherlands Railways at the time. These doors represented a major improvement from the draughty bus-style doors fitted to earlier rail buses but were destined to be unique to No. 140001.

This prototype was finished in BR's cooperate livery with the overall blue band around the window complimented by a grey band around the window area. When operating at speeds lower than 75 mph (121 km/h), No. 140001 had a distinct nodding motion and the ride quality was further reduced when the unit was operating on non-welded track and sharp bends. It appeared, therefore, at the time that BR was better off with its first generation DMUs than the proposed fleet of 140 styled rail buses. Remaining at Laira, Plymouth, until May 1986, No. 140001 was temporarily moved to Leeds Holbeck for storage until a final move to Leeds Neville Hill depot. BR considered using No. 140001 for driver training or a Sandite unit, but both proposals failed to materialise. In August 1994 a group of enthusiasts at the Keith & Dufftown Railway Association bought the unit from BR and it was eventually moved to Dufftown in February 1995.

The original two Class 150s were development trains, each fitted with a different power package for evaluation. All vehicles were powered with a full width driving cab in the outer end of each three-car set. The first of the build No. 150001 was fitted with one Cummins NT855 R5 engine rated at 285 hp (213 kw) driving a Voith 211 hydraulic transmission. Schneider final drive assemblies were provided. The second set No. 150002 was fitted originally with Rolls Royce Eagle C6 280HR engines rated at 280 hp (209 kw). Passenger accommodation was similar to the then recently built Class 455 EMUs for the Southern region. The bogies used under the design were a development of the successful BT13 family with secondary suspension using air bags. These incorporated a self-leveling valve for maintaining a standard floor height. Air-operated tread brakes using composite blocks rather than disc brakes were utilised. Fully automatic couplers were fitted instead of the tightlock design at the outer ends. This enabled units to be coupled/uncoupled without the need for shunting staff. Within units, vehicles were connected by semi-permanent bar couplers. The saloon heating used waste engine heat. The heaters were mounted under the seats with air distribution by electric fans. This system was supplemented by an oil-fired water heater. Carriage ventilators were incorporated in the roof and air circulation was aided by base-hinged passenger-operated twin hopper windows. The saloon lighting was by undiffused fluorescent tubes, longitudinally placed. Seating saloons were segregated from door vestibules by draught screens incorporating a toughened glass upper panel. A small lockable parcel or mail area was located in one driving car of each set. When this area was not required, seating using tip-up seats was provided. On the two prototype trains two different seating styles were installed. No. 150001 had bus-style seating with a mix of unidirectional and facing seats providing a total of 252. The crush loading capacity was estimated at 617. The middle vehicle of set No. 150002 originally incorporated a new BR inner suburban seating style which was not favoured by passengers in a market research study.

The original Class 150 concept design was deliberately flexible to accept a wide range of different interiors ranging from inward facing bench seats to InterCity luxury accommodation. The ratio of seats to standing room could be varied to suit individual operational requirements. A modular toilet compartment was installed in one vehicle of each unit. Authorisation was granted by the government to the BRB to order a further fifty Sprinter sets which were to be classified 150/1. Construction commenced immediately with deliveries taking place between October 1985 and March 1986 and the first sets were allocated to Derby Etches Park depot. The two prototype 150s came to Haymarket depot in July 1985 and were tested extensively around the Edinburgh area until the main fleet came to the depot the following year.

The second of the 'Super Sprinter' builds were the Class 156s, of which 114 two-car sets were built between 1987 and 1989 at Metro Cammell of Washwood Heath in Birmingham.

When introduced to Scotland in October 1988, they took over the Glasgow Central to Carlisle via the G&SW and Glasgow Central to Stranraer routes. However, many complaints were made including issues with overcrowding, poor leg and luggage space and limited toilet facilities. BR Scottish Region initially took on forty-eight sets split between Corkerhill, Haymarket and Inverness depots. By 2001 all units had been reallocated and based at Corkerhill depot after a further influx and transfers of Class 158 and 170 sets. A number of the Scottish allocated 156s were fitted with Radio Electronic Token Block (RETB) equipment, allowing operation over the West Highland and the Far North Lines. A number of liveries have been seen with several versions of the First ScotRail colours culminating in the application of the blue saltire livery based on the national flag of St Andrews. The original Strathclyde sets were numbered 156501–156514 and were initially provided with the standard orange livery. After a short period of operations with the Class 150–156 sets, more comfortable trains were still being sought by various train operators, including ScotRail. Roll forward the Class 158. However, with the ongoing electrification of Scotland's railways in the central belt, many have since migrated to Northern Rail and other operators.

By the late 1980s, the BRB was also looking to replace loco-hauled trains on the longer distance domestic routes. Following the successful introduction of the Class 150 and 156 units, a new specification to provide higher standards of performance and comfort with low running costs were sought. To give these units the maximum route availability, a massive aluminium assembly and fabrication plant was set up at BREL Derby Litchurch Lane works. The vast majority of the Class 158 units were built as two-car units and the fleet numbers ranged from 158701–158872, for standard units, and 158901–158910 for sets owned and operated by West Yorkshire PTE. ScotRail was the first area to introduce Class 158s, originally gaining forty-six sets in total. A small batch of units, Nos 158747–158751, were taken on board by InterCity to supplement its core fleet for low passengers on cross-country services. Considerable refurbishment and changes to liveries has taken place since privatisation. Class 158s featured full air conditioning, on board pay phone, power-operated interior doors, a toilet in each carriage and provision for stabling and plugging in a refurbishment trolley. The design was expected to achieve around 13,500 (21,725 km) of operation between major servicing and was expected to have an operating range of 1,600 miles between refueling. Despite the attention given to passenger facilities, the phrase 'garden shed engineering' was frequently used to describe the build. As a lightweight train and the first members of the Sprinter family to use disc brakes, autumn leaf mulch quickly built up on wheel trims and prevented trains from operating signalling track circuits correctly, while also affecting the braking. This was later solved by installing scrubbing blocks to clean the wheels. However, a temporary solution was required and in October 1992 a few sets were split and reformed into hybrid sets with Class 156 coaches. As time progressed the 158s also suffered from unreliable air conditioning systems, mainly due to the legal requirement of reducing CFC gases with which they were originally fitted with. This problem continued well after privatisation and many operators undertook major re-engineering or entire replacement of their air conditioning systems. The aluminium car body of the 158 lead to good route availability resulting in their ability to operate in most parts of the UK. However, some restrictions have been imposed due to clearance issues. From 2010, under the control of First Group, the Scottish allocated units began to work between Glasgow Central and Edinburgh via Shotts and on the Whifflet line. Some foreign 158s were also acquired to provide extra capacity on busier routes. Interiors on the Scottish sets have also seen refurbishment such as new seating, extra luggage space and new passenger information systems that have been fitted. Upgraded toilet retention tanks have also been fitted. Several of the 158s have been named. No. 158701 was named *BBC Scotland – 75 Years*, No. 158707 *Far North Line – 125th Anniversary*, No. 158715 *Haymarket* and No. 158720 was named *Inverness and Nairn Railway – 150 Years*.

Following on from the Class 168 design, which had been successful in England with Chiltern Railways, new trains were still being sought to cater for long-distance use. Based on the Class 168 design, part of the production facilities at Derby workshops was handed over to Turbostar production. These units later became Class 170 upwards. A total of 122 Class 170s were built. The first train operator to take on the Turbostars was Midland Main Line, working services from London St Pancras to Sheffield and Nottingham. After a period, these sets were replaced and were transferred to Central Trains, later London Midland and CrossCountry. ScotRail became the biggest user of Turbostars and at one time had a fleet of fifty-nine three-car sets being delivered between 1999 and 2005. The original sets were decked out in both first and standard class facilities. Later on, some interiors were changed, and this saw all standard class units dedicated to the Glasgow commuter area in Strathclyde PTE livery. All Class 170s were built to a common design with two pairs of bi-parting sliding plug doors on each side of each vehicle. A separate plug door was provided for each driving cab. Passenger doors fed a transverse walkway from where bi-parting doors led into the passenger saloons. Full air conditioning was provided as was Passenger Information Systems (PIS). All Turbostar stock is powered by one MTU 6R 183TD of 422 hp (315 kw) underfloor engine driving a Voith gearbox and ZF final drive. The maximum speed is 100 mph (161 km/h) and all sets are fitted with BSI auto couplers, allowing multiple working with members of the same class and the 14x and 15x types. They cannot operate in multiple with the 16x classes. Ownership of the entire Class 170 fleet rests with Peterbrook Leasing except a small batch, Nos 170416–170424, which are owned by Eversholt Leasing. The original ScotRail franchise taken on by National Express applied its own livery to the Class 170s followed by a repaint by First Group. This fleet then gained a new blue and white livery based on the Scottish Saltire after Transport Scotland announced in September 2008 that all trains would receive this livery.

After the creation of the First Transpenine Express Franchise, Siemens won the contract to provide fifty-six three-car Class 185 non-gangwayed sets at a cost of £260 million. They first began to appear on the Glasgow/Edinburgh to Manchester Airport service from December 2007 but started to be replaced by Class 350 EMUs from 2013. Originally ordered by Virgin Trains as part of their modernisation of the CrossCountry franchise, which was a requirement as part of the condition of the franchise award, Class 220 and 221 Voyagers were ordered to replace existing loco-hauled and high-speed trains (HST). However, once again these trains suffered and still suffer from criticism both from within and outside the rail industry as being inadequate for long-distance journeys. Today both the Class 220 and 221 sets have had their tilting capability removed and mainly operate with Virgin CrossCountry to supplement the Class 390 Pendolino fleet on the West Coast Main Line.

History – Class 150–221

Prototype

The prototype 'Sprinter', No. 150001, was a three-car DMU built by BREL in 1984.

Its first appearance in Scotland seems to be 16 May 1985, when it visited Glasgow Queen Street. The unit also came north to work a shuttle service from Edinburgh to the Haymarket depot open day on Saturday 24 August 1985. No. 150001's next spell in Scotland was longer. It formed a Glasgow–Oban special on 3 January 1986 to mark the opening of the new station building at Oban. The unit then spent six weeks based at Inverness depot, used on scheduled passenger services to Aberdeen, Kyle and Wick. On 17 February 1986 it was back in the West Highlands, working the 09:50 Glasgow–Fort William.

A second prototype unit was built by BREL, and while numbered as 154001 visited Scotland in 1987 for test runs.

Fleet Introduction

Haymarket depot got its first allocation of Sprinters in June 1987. Recently delivered Nos 150255/257/259 were sent from Newton Heath to Haymarket depot, to start staff training. Prior to use in regular service, the Sprinters were used on a number of excursions, taking them to fairly unusual destinations. Sprinters Nos 150255 and 150259 worked an Edinburgh–Stranraer excursion on 2 August for the 1987 Galloway Games. Another three units, Nos 150283–285, were newly delivered from York Works, ready for introduction on to the Edinburgh–Dundee and Edinburgh–Bathgate routes from October 1987. Further units were sent to Haymarket from October 1988 until, by May 1989, the fleet was up to eighteen units, ready for introduction on to the Edinburgh–Dunblane, North Berwick and Dunbar, and the new Fife Circle services.

The 1990s

In 1991 the Edinburgh–Dundee service was extended to Aberdeen using Class 158s, and two surplus 150s were sent to Cardiff. Two further units were exchanged for Class 156s in 1994. On 25 March 1996, No. 150285 was named *Edinburgh-Bathgate 1986–1996* to celebrate the tenth anniversary of the line reopening. It carried this name until the end of November 2004. Introduction of the second batch of Class 170 Turbostars, and cascading of Class 158s onto local services, saw two units sent south in the autumn of 2000. During the winter of 2000/1, the remaining twelve units were overhauled at Glasgow Works and turned out in the ScotRail Railways white and purple livery, strangely with a narrower green stripe than other classes. In addition to the regular Fife, Bathgate and Dunblane work, the 150s sometimes visited Glasgow Queen Street. The class also made occasional appearances on the Edinburgh–West Calder–Glasgow Central route. The final twelve Class 150s were displaced by Suburban Class 170s funded by the Scottish Executive. The units lasted just long enough to see in the First ScotRail era and get new branding. The first to depart was No. 150256 on 16 November 2004, and the last was No. 150258, which headed south on 4 March 2005. All these units went to Cardiff, although three units spent some weeks on loan to Neville Hill depot (Leeds).

Former ScotRail Fleet

Unit (No.)	Departed	Reallocated
150208	10, Dec. 2004	to Neville Hill, then Cardiff.
150228	Autumn 2000	to Neville Hill.
150244	20, Sep. 1991	to Cardiff, then Exeter.
150245	Autumn 2000	to Neville Hill, then Norwich, then Cardiff, then Exeter.
150248	20, Sep. 1991	to Cardiff, then Exeter.
150250	07, Feb. 2005	to Cardiff.
150252	21, Jan. 2005	to Cardiff.
150255	28, Feb. 1994	to Tyseley, then Norwich, then Tyseley.
150256	16, Nov. 2004	to Neville Hill, then Cardiff.
150257	14, Mar. 1994	to Tyseley, then Norwich, then Tyseley.
150258	04, Mar. 2005	to Cardiff.
150259	03, Dec. 2004	to Cardiff.
150260	21, Jan. 2005	to Cardiff.
150262	26, Nov. 2004	to Cardiff.
150264	04, Jan. 2005	to Cardiff.
150283	20, Dec. 2004	to Cardiff.
150284	24, Nov. 2004	to Neville Hill, then Cardiff.
150285	11, Feb. 2005	to Cardiff.

Works Visitors
Class 150 units based in England have visited various Works for overhaul or repair. Hunslet Barclay at Kilmarnock refurbished and repainted (Nos 150133–150 and 150201–03/05–07/11/15–18/22–25) for First North Western from 1999–2000. RailCare at Springburn refurbished and repainted seven units for Silverlink in 2000 (units 150120/23/27–31), Brodie Rail at Kilmarnock, repaired No. 150135 for Northern Rail in 2014.

Track Recording Unit
Network Rail owns the Track Recording Unit No. 950001 (999600 + 999601), which was purpose-built in 1987 based on the Class 150/1 design. This unit has carried several different liveries in its career. It has been in all yellow since 2005.

Class 156 Units

This fleet was originally split between SPT sponsored services and other ScotRail services. As such, twenty-eight of them were in SPT Carmine and Cream livery, and twenty in First ScotRail blue livery. With the transfer of SPT's rail powers to Transport Scotland and the rebranding of the ScotRail franchise to a unified livery, the entire fleet of twenty-eight Carmine and Cream 156s was repainted into the new ScotRail saltire livery.

Radio Electronic Tokenless Block (RETB)
Fifteen of the 'blue' units are fitted with RETB equipment for working on the West Highland Line. These are Nos 156447, 156450, 156453, 156456, 156457, 156458, 156465, 156467, 156474, 156476, 156485, 156493 and 156499. Nos 156462 and 156496 had it removed.

In early 2014, two 'SPT' units numbered 156445 and 156500 were fitted with the equipment. Unit 156478 also had RETB equipment removed during 2015 but was refitted following the completion of refurbishment. In October 2016, No. 156478 returned to service after suffering derailment damage at Mauchline, after running into severe flooding. This unit was also involved in a derailment near Girvan on the Stranraer line in 2002 and sustained numerous other incidents when based at Inverness working the Kyle and Far North Lines. It is now owned by Brodies of Kilmarnock.

First ScotRail Refurbishment
The ScotRail 156s went through a refurbishment programme at Derby Works with No. 156450 being the first to get the treatment, returning in February 2007. The refurbishment programme was completed in November 2007. From 2016–present ScotRail Class 156 units visited Glasgow Works to receive upgraded modifications including the fitting of a disabled toilet. This work also involves a full repaint and will eventually include a full interior refresh including new Fainsa seats, power sockets and lights. Unit Nos 156430 to 156433, 156436, 156439, 156442, 156462, 156467, 156494, 156501 to 156514 were completed, along with Brodies refurbished and owned No. 156478. Currently Nos 156430, 156431, 156433, 156436, 156439, 156442, 156494, 156504 and 156510 are the ones with the full refurbishment. Hopefully the entire project should be completed by 2020.

Routes
Class 156s currently operate the following routes:
Glasgow Queen Street–Oban/Fort William/Mallaig (RETB fitted units only). Glasgow Queen Street/Edinburgh–Stirling/Dunblane/Alloa (shared with 158s/170s).
Glasgow Queen Street–Falkirk Grahamston (shared with the 158s/170s).
Glasgow Queen Street–Maryhill–Anniesland (shared with 158s/170s).
Edinburgh–Carstairs–Motherwell–Glasgow Central (Shared with 380s).
Fife Circle (more commonly covered by 158s/170s).
Glasgow Central–East Kilbride.
Glasgow Central–Barrhead.
Glasgow Central–Kilmarnock.
Glasgow Central–Dumfries–Carlisle/Newcastle.
Glasgow Central–Stranraer.
Stranraer/Girvan/Ayr–Kilmarnock/Newcastle
Class 156s can also occasionally be found on the following lines in the event of service disruption:
Glasgow Central/Edinburgh Waverley – North Berwick/Dunbar (more commonly covered by Class 158/Class 170).
Edinburgh Waverley/Glasgow Queen Street–Perth/Dundee (more commonly covered by Class 158/Class 170).

Class 158s

ScotRail operate a fleet of forty Class 158 Express DMUs. These are allocated between Haymarket depot and Inverness depot. The units are primarily used on long-distance rural services as well as short distance commuter services within the Central Belt.

Routes
Class 158s currently operate the following routes:
Glasgow Queen Street/Edinburgh – Stirling/Dunblane/Alloa (shared with 156s/170s).
Glasgow Queen Street–Falkirk Grahamston (shared with the 156s/170s).

Glasgow Queen Street–Maryhill–Anniesland (shared with 156s/170s).
Edinburgh Waverley/Glasgow Queen Street–Perth/Dundee/Aberdeen/Inverness (shared with 170s).
Aberdeen–Inverness (shared with 170s).
Inverness–Kyle/Wick.
Fife Circle (shared with 156s/170s).

Refurbishment

The Class 158s underwent an exterior repainting programme from First ScotRail livery into the ScotRail Saltire livery. This was completed in 2018.

Loans

Nos 158782, 158786, 158789 and 159791 arrived at HA on loan during February 2007. No. 158791 returned south to Northern on 3 March 2007 while the other three units remained and have now been repainted into the TS ScotRail Saltire livery. Nos 158867, 158868, 158869 and 158870 arrived at Haymarket on 14 December 2007 on long-term loan from Northern, an arrangement which was due to end in June 2010. However, a new agreement was made with the ROSCO and the units remained with Abellio ScotRail until 2018, when Class 385 EMUs started to arrive. They were then transferred to Northern Rail.

Class 170 Turbostars

At one time ScotRail had a fleet of fifty-nine Class 170 Turbostars, all based at Haymarket depot in Edinburgh. An initial order for twenty-four three-car units (Nos 170401–424) was placed with Adtranz in 1999, when ScotRail were under the tenure of National Express. A further two units (Nos 170470 and 170471) were received as part of a compensation deal with the manufacturer. Ten more units numbered as 170425–434 followed in 2003/4. These make up the Express pool along with the initial twenty-four units. In 2004/5, the seven SPT pool units (Nos 170472–478) and twelve Suburban units (Nos 170450–461) were delivered. In 2017, units 170421–424 were transferred to Southern and have since been renumbered to Class 171s. In 2018 sixteen Class 170s were transferred to Northern Rail, these were units 170453–61 and 170472–8.

Class 170 Express Pool

The Class 170 Express Pool forms the mainstay of the 170 fleet and the units see heavy use on services between Edinburgh, Glasgow, Aberdeen, Inverness, Perth and Dundee. Peak time services between Edinburgh and Glasgow are diagrammed for pairs of Express 170s. First class accommodation was provided as built. All units are now painted in Scotland's Railway livery but in the process of being replaced by Class 43 HST and MK3 coaches.

Class 170 Buffet Pool

In 2005 First ScotRail acquired four Turbostars from Hull Trains. When they arrived, these units were operated in Hull Trains green and white but were quickly repainted into standard First ScotRail livery. The interior fittings of these units differed from ScotRail's in a number of ways, most notable is the provision of a buffet counter in the centre coach. These sets are not operated on dedicated diagrams and can be found on any Class 170 working. All of the 170/3s are in the saltire livery. From late 2017, all of the 170/3s had their buffet counters removed in place for more seats.

Class 170 Suburban Pool

Twelve suburban units mainly operate Fife local services as well as Edinburgh to Tweedmouth and Dunblane services. Initially, the Suburban pool units were kept to the above diagrams as much as possible as first class accommodation was not provided. The units have now been fitted out with first class except Nos 170458/59/60/61, as per the Express pool, and can therefore be used on any class 170 diagram. All these units now all wear the 'Saltire' livery.

Class 170 SPT Pool

Seven Class 170s did initially wear SPT livery with non-standard green and orange interiors. These units formerly worked almost exclusively on SPT sponsored Glasgow Queen Street to Stirling/Dunblane/Cumbernauld/Falkirk Grahamston services. However, the units are now maintained and operated by Abellio Scotrail since the SPT ceased having any say over rail operations in the former Glasgow PTE area. These units can be used on any Class 170 diagrams, although first class is not provided. These seven units have now been received the 'Saltire' livery with No. 170478 being the last in the SPT colours being repainted in May 2014. Nos 170475–8 were transferred to Northern Rail in March 2018.

One Offs

Class 170s have occasionally operated as two-car sets when the centre coach (fifty-six car) fails on an otherwise healthy unit. No. 170401 was delivered in this manner with No. 56401 in its formation, in addition to 56402. Another four-car set was formed in July 2000 when No. 56408 was inserted into No. 170407 and again in November 2000 when the center coach from No. 170412 was inserted into unit No. 170417. Two units briefly carried advertising liveries in 1999. No. 170414 carried a special silver livery, promoting *The Herald* newspaper, while No. 170415 was decked out in dark blue with orange spots advertising the *Sunday Herald* ('No ordinary trainspotter'). The adverts covered the centre coach of each unit.

In Spring 2015, No. 170414 was painted in a special livery to promote the reopening of the Borders Railway in September 2015. In Summer 2007, Nos 170420 and 170421 were re-vinyled into 'Back The Bid' colours to support the City of Glasgow's ultimately successful bid for the 2014 Commonwealth Games. The vinyl was predominantly light blue with brown doors and was also used by a number of Glasgow subway trains.

In January 2012, No. 170433 suffered cab damage after running into a tree during a winter storm. To replace the damaged car, the 50 coach from No. 170425 was added to the set from the tenth of the month until the 1 February. Notably, the latter coach was painted in the blue Saltire livery, while the 79 and 56 cars of No. 170433 wore barbie livery. A second hybrid set was formed on the second of February using No. 50425, this time paired with barbie-liveried Nos 56453 and 79453. The formations were corrected in April 2012.

The three-car 185s TransPennine units work the vast majority of First TransPennine Express's services in the north of England. From December 2007 these units started to operate between Manchester Airport and Glasgow/Edinburgh. The first visit of a Class 185 in Scotland was when Siemens took a set to Stirling for a conference on the 7 February 2007.

It operated as the 6X79 14:48 Mossend Yard–Stirling. No. 185138 had arrived at Mossend just after 03:00 behind No. 67006. The Royal locomotive changed ends so it would be leading on the return run and this meant No. 67030 led for the run up to Stirling, arriving just after 15:40 into platform 10. The return run 6X80 20:20 Stirling to the South now saw No. 67006 leading the train with No. 67030 tailing on the rear. It left Stirling eight minutes down at 20:28. Class 185s worked on a number of training runs to Scotland in the weeks leading up to the start of First TransPennine Express's Manchester services, initially to Glasgow and then to Edinburgh.

Class 220 and 221s operate between Glasgow/Edinburgh and the South via Birmingham. They also work some trains north of Edinburgh to Dundee and Aberdeen. Initially they operated on the WCML to Manchester and Birmingham. They were built by Bombardier and delivered between 2001 and 2002. They are based at Central Rivers depot, near Burton-on-Trent. Each Class 220 vehicle has a 750 hp Cummins QSK1 diesel engine under the floor, which powers two electric traction motors driving the inner axles on each bogie. The trains have a maximum speed of 125 mph. Class 220s are very similar to Class 221s. However, the two classes are fitted with different bogies; the Class 220s have inside frames, which expose the whole of the wheel face. When operated by Virgin CrossCountry, the 220s had a 'silver shield' on the nose and red-backed nameplates. All the units were named, prior to Virgin losing the WCML franchise. Class 220 units have visited the Bo'ness & Kinneil Railway to carry out autumn low adhesion training for Virgin Trains drivers. Unit 220009 *Gatwick Voyager* was the first of the class to visit on 28 September 2001. It was the last training run of the season, the other trips had used 158s. Training with Class 220s also took place for three weeks in September 2002, with units running from Edinburgh to Cadder Yard to reverse before heading to Bo'ness. On a semi-regular basis Class 220 and 221 units have been diverted off the WCML via Cathcart and diverted over the G&SW lines via Kilmarnock and Dumfries during periods of engineering works.

After franchise changes on the 10 November 2007, the fleet was split between Arriva CrossCountry and Virgin West Coast. Class 221s now operate for Virgin West Coast between Glasgow Central/Edinburgh Waverley and Birmingham New Street. Arriva CrossCountry routes are via the East Coast Main Line and Birmingham to/from Dundee and Aberdeen. The 221s have tilting bogies which they can use on the West Coast Main Line to achieve speeds up to 125 mph, where non-tilting trains are restricted to lower speeds. Up until the 2007 franchise changes, all the units were named, mostly after famous explorers. Some retain their name still. Unit 221105 *William Baffin* visited Glasgow Queen Street station on the evening of 10 December 2003. This was a test to see if the axle counter train detection system used in the Queen Street area was compatible with the train's Tilt Authorisation and Speed Supervision (TASS) system. The train ran from Carstairs to Glasgow Queen Street via Coatbridge Central and Springburn. The return ran from Queen Street to Eastfield Loop, then Springburn, Coatbridge Central, Rutherglen and Polmadie depot.

Depot codes:

AK – Ardwick Manchester
CK – Corkerhill (Glasgow)
CZ – Central Rivers Barton Under Needwood
GW – Shields Glasgow
HA – Haymarket
HT – Heaton
HQ – Headquarters (BR)
IS – Inverness
NH – Newton Heath Manchester
NL – Neville Hill Leeds
ZA – RTC Derby
Information supplied by Willie Carlyle of Ayr depot. (BR)

No. 156432 (CK) south of Stewarton with a Glasgow Central to Kilmarnock local service. This track was singled in June 1974 and still causes operational delays to ScotRail services today. Taken in March 2010.

Four-car No. 143019 (HQ), at Edinburgh Waverley ready to depart with a service to Bathgate. Taken in April 1986.

Three-car 150 prototype No. 001 (HQ) departs from Ayr with a special train from Glasgow Central to Stranraer Harbour. This was being tested out to replace Class 47s and Mk II stock. Taken in March 1988.

Two-car 141 (NH) lies in Barclays Yard Kilmarnock, now owned by Wabtec, awaiting a move into the works for modification work. Taken in June 1989.

No. 170405 (HA) approaches Montrose South with the 10:40 Glasgow Queen Street to Aberdeen service. Note how excited the driver appears to be! Taken in June 2001.

No. 158768 (NL) at Glasgow Central. This set had worked into Glasgow from Leeds via the Settle & Carlisle route. This service was provided by TransPenine but only lasted for six years. Taken in January 2000.

Five-car 221 at Carstairs with a Birmingham New Street to Edinburgh service. Taken in March 2004.

No. 150225 (NH) at Glasgow Central platform 1. This unit had worked from Preston instead of a failed Class 86 and Mk II rolling stock. Taken in July 1987.

No. 156496 (CK) lies in platform 1 Glasgow Queen Street awaiting another run to Maryhill. The empty siding on the left was not relaid when Queen Street was upgraded for electric traction in 2016. Taken in May 2001.

Four-car No. 156506 (CK) departs from Lugton heading to Kilmarnock with a Branch Line Special. It had just come up from Giffen and reversed. Taken in August 1992.

No. 156457 (IS) on the jacks inside Inverness depot receiving repairs. This unit was later transferred to Corkerhill depot in August 2000. Taken in February 2000.

Six car 158/150 combination of empty coaching stock arrives at Edinburgh Waverley. The 158 would work a Dundee service after detaching and the rear four-car 150s would probably work local Fife Circle services. Taken in April 2002.

Six-car No. 170408 (HA) leading at Edinburgh with the 08:00 service to Glasgow Queen Street. Taken in April 2002.

No. 156474 (CK) at Woodhill, north of Kilmarnock, with the 11:12 Carlisle to Glasgow Central service. Taken in March 2004.

No. 170406 (HA) with a fitter at platform 3 Glasgow Queen Street, having just arrived with a service from Dundee. Taken in September 2000.

Four-car No. 150252 (HA) emerges out of the sun at Edinburgh Waverley with a local Outer Circle service for Fife. Taken in April 2002.

No. 156465 (CK) arrives at Greenfaulds station with a Cumbernauld to Glasgow Queen Street service. Taken in October 2002.

No. 170413 (HA) arrives in the sub platform Edinburgh Waverley with a Cowdenbeath to Newcraighall service. Taken in June 2003.

No. 156430 (CK) approaches Girvan station with a Stranraer Harbour to Glasgow Central service. These direct services were routed to/from Kilmarnock from May 2017. Any passengers for stations north of Ayr now have to change at Ayr station onto an electric service. Taken in June 2006.

Five-car 221 (CZ) at the old platform 11 at Edinburgh Waverley with a CrossCountry service to Birmingham New Street via the ECML. Taken in March 2004.

No. 158802 (NH) departs Glasgow Central with the 14:12 service to Leeds via the Carlisle & Settle line. Taken in November 2002.

No. 158728 (HA) in the bay platfoms, Perth, having arrived with a service from Edinburgh via Ladybank. Taken in August 1998.

Five-car 221 arrives in the mid road Kilmarnock with a diverted Birmingham New Street to Glasgow Central service. This service was diverted due to engineering work on the West Coast Main Line at Lockerbie. Taken in February 2004.

Four-car 156s, 509 (CK) at the front, in the north bay platforms Carlisle. This unit would work the 13:12 service to Glasgow Central, the rear unit would work a local service to Dumfries. Taken in November 2002.

No. 158737 (HA) at Edinburgh Waverley having just arrived with a service from Kirkcaldy. This unit was transferred from Haymarket to Cardiff Canton in May 2000. Taken in August 1998.

No. 170407 (HA) purrs past Edinburgh Park station with the 10:00 service from Glasgow Queen Street to Edinburgh service. Taken in March 2004.

No. 158717 (IS) approaches Rose Street Inverness with a morning service from Kyle Of Lochlash. Taken in June 2004.

No. 158725 (IS) arrives at Linlithgow with the 10:50 Edinburgh to Dunblane service. Taken in March 2004.

No. 170419 (HA) emerges out of Haymarket Tunnel to the station with the 10:15 Edinburgh to Glasgow Queen Street service. Taken in March 2004.

No. 156453 (CK) seen at Eastfield depot before the yard had was electrified. This unit was at the sidings to be refueled between West Highland Duties. Taken in March 2007.

No. 170429 (HA) at Haymarket with the 10:30 Edinburgh to Glasgow Queen Street service. Taken in March 2004.

No. 158732 (HA) approaches Polmont with a morning service to Dunblane. Taken in March 2004.

No. 150284 (HA) approaches Edinburgh Park station with an Edinburgh to Stirling service. Note Arthur's Seat at Edinburgh in the background. This hill near Edinburgh castle is 822 feet high (250.5 m). Taken in March 2004.

No. 156513 (CK) arrives at Kennishead station with the 13:57 Glasgow Central to Barrhead service. Taken in March 2012.

No. 170453 (HA) at platform 1 with a service to North Berwick. Taken in August 2005.

Five-car 221 near Newton station with a northbound service from Newcastle to Glasgow Central. Taken in March 2004.

Two-car 156 crosses Ballochmyle Viaduct, south of Mauchline, with the 17:36 Newcastle to Stranraer Harbour service. Taken in May 2005.

No. 150208 (HA) at Inverkeithing with an Edinburgh to Markinch service. Taken in May 2002.

No. 158713 (IS) approaches Edinburgh Park station with a Bathgate to Edinburgh service. Taken in March 2004.

No. 170409 (HA) at Maryhill station departs with a service from Glasgow Queen Street to Anniesland. Taken in July 2006.

Four-car 220 passes Mussleburgh station with a southbound service from Edinburgh to Penzance. Taken in June 2004.

No. 158713 (IS) arrives at Dyce with the 11:26 Inverurie to Aberdeen service. Note the rig workers in the bus shelters, having just arrived off the helicopter at the nearby airport. Taken in June 2004.

No. 156474 (CK) at Craigens near Cumnock with the 15:12 Carlisle to Glasgow Central service. Taken in May 2005.

Five-car 221 arrives at Edinburgh with a service from Sheffield. Taken in August 2005.

No. 156442 (CK) at Ballochmyle, near Mauchline, with the 11:10 Carlisle to Glasgow Central service. Taken in January 2011.

Two-car departmental Class 150 No. 950001 (ZA) passes Falkland Yard Ayr with a northbound working. This unit was specifically built for departmental use and used for track assessment work. Taken in May 2006.

Four-car No. 158707 *Far North Line 125th Anniversary* (IS) arrives on the rear of ECS from Haymarket depot to form the 13:25 service to Inverness. Taken in August 2005.

No. 156431 (CK) approaches Lugton with the 09:27 Kilmarnock to Glasgow Central service. The disconnected line in the foreground was the freight-only branch to Giffen. This was truncated in October 2009 when doubling of the main line from Lugton to Stewarton took place. Taken in March 2010.

No. 156485 (CK) at Kelvindale with the 10:20 Anniesland to Glasgow Queen Street service. This station was reopened in September 2005. Taken in September 2018.

No. 158786 (HA) departs from Haymarket station heading to the nearby Haymarket depot with ECS from Edinburgh. This unit had been transferred from South West trains and was eventually repainted in ScotRail saltire livery in 2009. Taken in April 2006.

No. 170404 (HA) at Aberdeen ready to depart with a service to Edinburgh. Taken in June 2004.

No. 156436 (CK) departs Linlithgow with an Edinburgh to Dunblane service. Taken in March 2004.

No. 221138 *Thor Heyerdahl* (CZ) at platform 6 at Glasgow Central with a CrossCountry service to Birmingham New Street. Taken in July 2006.

No. 158741 (HA) at Anniesland having just arrived with the 10:48 service from Glasgow Queen Street. Taken in July 2006.

No. 156445 (CK) at Blackfaulds Cutting, near Cumnock, with the 09:58 Glasgow Central to Carlisle service. Taken in February 2008.

No. 158734 (HA) at Dunblane with the 11:38 to Edinburgh service. Taken in July 2009.

No. 170413 (HA) at Newcraighall having just arrived with a service from Kirkcaldy. Taken in June 2003.

No. 156510 (CK) at Stirling with the 09:38 Dunblane to Edinburgh service. Taken in September 2007.

No. 158741 (HA) at Springburn with the 13:33 Glasgow Queen Street to Falkirk Grahamston service. Taken in May 2012.

No. 170475 (HA) in Strathclyde livery approaches Larbert with the 10:37 Glasgow Queen Street to Stirling service. Taken in September 2007.

No. 185128 (AK) at Edinburgh Waverley with the 13:50 TransPennine service to Manchester Airport. Taken in November 2007.

No. 158736 (HA) stabled in Whifflet Sidings, near Coatbridge, between duties. The unit had arrived with a service from Glasgow Central. These services are now worked by electrics, mainly Class 318 and 320s. This line also allows trains to run from Whifflet to join the Northclyde lines at Sunnyside Junction. Taken in June 2012.

No. 170421 (HA) arrives at Polmont with the 12:30 Glasgow Queen Street to Edinburgh service. Taken in March 2004.

No. 170474 (HA) at Stirling with the 10:18 Glasgow Queen Street to Alloa service. This line was electrified in 2018 when diesels were mainly replaced by electrics. Taken in June 2008.

No. 156445 (CK) at Dumbreck with the 14:42 Glasgow Central to Paisley Canal service. These services went over to electrics from December 2012. Taken in May 2012.

Six-car 170, unit 417 (HA) trailing, departs Edinburgh Waverley with the 13:00 service to Glasgow Queen Street. Taken in November 2007.

No. 156513 (CK) at Stewarton with the 11:12 Carlisle to Glasgow Central service. In the background work was underway to redouble the line to allow for a new half-hourly service starting from December 2009. Taken in August 2009.

No. 170433 (HA) arrives at Dundee with the 11:50 Aberdeen to Edinburgh service. Taken in November 2008.

No. 156509 (CK) at Bank Junction, north of New Cumnock, with the 12:36 Newcastle to Stranraer Harbour service. Taken in April 2009.

No. 170459 (HA) arrives at Glasgow Queen Street with the 10:05 service from Falkirk Grahamston. Taken in May 2009.

No. 156462 (CK) approaches Kilmaurs with the 13:12 Glasgow Central to Carlisle service. This line was omitted from the redoubling project in 2009 and still causes major congestion and delays. Taken in March 2010.

No. 158728 (HA) approaches Larbert station with the 10:55 Dunblane to Edinburgh service. Taken in September 2007.

No. 170475 (HA) arrives in Dunblane from the nearby sidings to form the 12:20 Dunblane to Glasgow Queen Street service. Taken in September 2007.

No. 158725 (IS) approaches Haymarket station with a service from Bathgate. Taken in August 2009.

Four-car 156, unit 467 (CK) leading, at Lugton with the 07:32 Kilmarnock to Glasgow Central service. The former connecting line from Neilston can just about be made out coming in from the left. Taken in April 2010.

No. 158728 (HA) arrives at Perth with a local service from Edinburgh. Taken in August 1998.

No. 156477 (CK) at Hillhouse near Barassie with the 11:05 Kilmarnock to Girvan service. Taken in April 2010.

No. 221113 (CZ) arrives at Haymarket with a Dundee to Paignton service. Taken in June 2008.

No. 156503 (CK) near Cumnock with the 11:07 Carlisle to Glasgow Central service. Taken in September 2009.

No. 158739 (IIA) at Bathgate old station with the 13.18 service from Edinburgh Waverley. This platform closed on commencement of a resited station in connection with the new electric service from December 2010. Taken in November 2009.

No. 158867 (HA) approaches Haymarket with a Fife circular service. At the time this unit was in Alphaline livery. This unit had been transferred from Neville Hill depot Leeds in December 2007. Taken in August 2009.

Modified 150 unit No. 950001 (ZA) waits in the mid road at Kilmarnock with a Network Rail track assessment train en route from Carlisle Kingmoor to Mossend Yard. Taken in January 2010.

Four-car 156, 512 (CK) leading, approaches Dunlop with the 08:28 Glasgow Central to Carlisle and Girvan service. Taken in February 2010.

No. 170478 (HA) approaches Edinburgh with ECS from Haymarket depot to form a North Berwick service. Most of these services are electric apart from the odd diesel working. Taken in August 2005.

No. 170450 (HA) at Glasgow Queen Street having just arrived with a service from Aberdeen. Taken in May 2009.

Two-car 156 crosses over the river Irvine on Carmel Viaduct, near Kilmaurs, with the 11:57 Kilmarnock to Glasgow Central service. Taken in March 2010.

No. 170416 (HA) departs Haymarket station with the 13:40 Edinburgh to Aberdeen service. Taken in August 2009.

No. 156476 (CK) at Dumbarton Central with the 08:08 Arrochar to Glasgow Queen Street service. Taken in May 2018.

No. 158723 (IS) departs Edinburgh with ECS to Haymarket depot via the sub line. Note the car park in the foreground. This was later converted to two additional platforms to increase capacity at the east end of the station. Taken in August 2005.

No. 156430 (CK) at Kilwinning with the Sunday 12:10 Stranraer Harbour to Glasgow Central service. Taken in May 2010.

Four-car 156 crosses Stewarton Viaduct with the 09:03 Glasgow Central to Girvan service. Taken in June 2010.

No. 156437 (CK) at Bonnyton, on the outskirts of Kilmarnock, with a service from Glasgow Central. Note the person in the rear – not the driver but the conductor. Signal K76 gives drivers five route options at Kilmarnock station. Taken in April 2010.

No. 158727 (IS) at Kirkwood with the 11:28 Whifflet to Glasgow Central service. Taken in May 2011.

No. 221125 (CZ) departs from Glasgow Central with an Arriva CrossCountry service to Paignton. Taken in June 2011.

No. 156511 (CK) arrives at platform 4 Kilmarnock with the 10:03 Glasgow Central to Carlisle service. Note the Johnnie Walker whisky factory in the background in the process of being demolished. Taken in January 2013.

No. 156430 (CK) at Garrochburn between Mauchline and Kilmarnock with the 07:56 Newcastle to Glasgow Central service. Taken in October 2011.

No. 170424 (HA) at platform 11 at Edinburgh, ready to depart with the 11:45 service to Glasgow Queen Street. Taken in April 2006.

No. 158786 (HA) approaches Glasgow Central with the 14:58 service from Whifflet. Taken in June 2011.

No. 156508 (CK) arrives at Auchinleck with the 13:03 Glasgow Central to Carlisle service. Taken in June 2012.

Five-car 221 arrives at Glasgow Central with a service from Birmingham New Street. Taken in June 2012.

No. 185134 (AK) departs Haymarket with the 10:55 Edinburgh to Manchester Airport service. Taken in June 2008.

No. 156506 (CK) takes on its next load of passengers at East Kilbride with the 12:07 service to Glasgow Central. Taken in June 2012.

No. 170411 (HA) arrives at Cumbernauld with the 11:18 Falkirk Grahamston to Glasgow Queen Street service. Taken in June 2012.

No. 156505 (CK) approaches Priesthill and Darnley station with the 14:17 Barrhead to Glasgow Central service. Taken in January 2013.

No. 158751 (NH) arrives at Glasgow Central with a morning service from Preston. This was on a Virgin CrossCountry service before being reallocated to Tyseley depot in January 2002. Taken in May 1998.

No. 185149 (AK) passes Carstairs with the 08:10 Manchester Airport to Glasgow Central service. Note the northbound Freightliner in the Down loop. Taken in March 2013.

No. 158717 (IS) at Brodies Engineering Kilmarnock. The unit was in for minor repairs. Taken in April 2013.

No. 156449 (CK) at Lochside, north of New Cumnock, with the 09:12 Glasgow Central to Carlisle service. Taken in April 2013.

Ten-car 221 Voyager class at Mossband, just south of the border, with the 10:40 Glasgow Central to London Euston via Birmingham New Street service. Taken in May 2013.

No. 156434 (CK) at Bowhouse, south of Hurlford, with the 10:03 Glasgow Central to Carlisle service. Taken in August 2013.

No. 170427 (HA) arrives at Lenzie with the 10:15 Glasgow Queen Street to Edinburgh service. Taken in May 2013.

No. 156512 (CK) at Ballieston with the 09:20 Glasgow Central to Whifflet service. These services went over to electrics from December 2014. Taken in May 2014.

No. 1568728 (HA) arrives at Gartcosh with the 12:50 Cumbernauld to Glasgow Queen Street service. Note the X sticker on the non-driver's window. This indicates that there was a defect with the coupler preventing the unit being coupled up to another unit until repairs carried out at a depot. Taken in May 2013.

No. 156493 (CK) at Hairmyres station with the 13:48 Glasgow Central to East Kilbride service. Taken in November 2013.

No. 158868 (HA) arrives at a misty Edinburgh Park with the 12:03 Edinburgh to Dunblane service. Taken in November 2013.

No. 156430 (CK) at Busby with the 13:48 Glasgow Central to East Kilbride service. Beyond this point the line is single with only a crossing loop at Hairmyres. Taken in November 2013.

No. 170453 (HA) arrives at Croy with the 09:30 Glasgow Queen Street to Edinburgh service. Taken in May 2013.

No. 158740 (HA) arrives at Edinburgh with the 10:13 service from Cowdenbeath. Taken in February 2014.

Arriva CrossCountry No. 221133 (AK) arrives at Motherwell with the 13:10 Glasgow Central to Birmingham New Street service. Taken in February 2014.

No. 156467 (CK) is seen north of Lugton with the 14:13 Glasgow Central to Kilmarnock service. Taken in April 2014.

No. 156449 (CK) approaches Carmyle and crosses under the M74 motorway with the 09:08 Whifflet to Glasgow Central service. Taken in May 2014.

No. 170472 (HA) at Bishopbriggs with the 10:18 Glasgow Queen Street to Stirling service. Taken in May 2013.

Five-car 221 emerges from the east end of Edinburgh at the Mound Tunnel with a CrossCountry service from Sheffield. Taken in August 2005.

No. 170478 (HA) at Glasgow Central having just arrived with a diverted service from Aberdeen. This was during the closure of Glasgow Queen Street for electrification work. Taken in June 2016.

Six-car 156, unit 453 (CK) leading, at Bowling with the 12:42 Glasgow Queen Street to Oban and Mallaig service. Normally the front four coaches detach at Crianlarich for Fort William/Mallaig and the rear two go to Oban. Taken in September 2014.

No. 156505 (CK) approaches Kirkhill station with a diverted Glasgow Central to Edinburgh via Shotts service. This service was diverted due to engineering work at Polmadie. Taken in January 1995.

No. 170456 (HA) near Springburn station, between Cowlairs North and West Junctions, with the 11:18 Falkirk Grahamston to Glasgow Queen Street service. Taken in June 2015.

No. 156502 (CK) near Hairmyres with the 12:12 Glasgow Central to East Kilbride service. Taken in July 2015.

No. 221111 (AK) at Kilmarnock with a diverted Glasgow Central to Carlisle service. This was due to the WCML being closed at Lamington station due to structural damage to Lamington Viaduct. Taken in January 2016.

No. 170470 (HA) at Glasgow Queen Street with the 11:18 service to Stirling. Taken in June 2000.

158733 (HA) at Stow on the reopened Waverley route with the 10:05 Edinburgh to Tweedbank service. Taken in October 2015.

No. 158708 (IS) arrives at Glasgow Central platform 3 with a service from Edinburgh via Shotts. Taken in February 2015.

No. 170401 (HA) emerges out of the gloom of the Glasgow Queen Street tunnel and climbs up the 1 in 40 gradient towards Cowlairs with the 12:15 service to Edinburgh. Taken in August 2015.

No. 158867 (HA) on the rear of a four-car service, passing Bellgrove with a diverted Falkirk Grahamston to Glasgow Queen Street Low Level service. Taken in June 2016.

No. 154001 (HQ) at Glasgow Queen Street with a train from Aberdeen. This was utilised instead of the normal Class 47/Mk II coaches. Needless to say, most of the passengers on board were less than impressed. Taken in May 1987.

Five-car 221 at Ochiltree near Ballochmyle with a diverted Carlisle to Glasgow Central service. Taken in February 2016.

No. 158760 (NL) at Glasgow Central with the 14:00 service to Leeds via the Carlisle & Settle line. Taken in June 2001.

Four-car 220 approaches Shieldmuir, south of Motherwell, with an Arriva CrossCountry service from Glasgow Central to Birmingham New Street. Taken in March 2016.

No. 170408 (HA) on the rear of a six-car service at Glasgow Queen Street Low Level to Edinburgh via Springburn. This was due to the high level station being closed in connection with electrification work. Taken in June 2016.

Five-car 221, south of
New Cumnock, with
a diverted Glasgow
Central to Carlisle
service. Taken in
January 2016.

No. 170402 (HA)
departs Dundee with
the 13:36 Aberdeen
to Edinburgh service.
Taken in June 2001.

No. 170427 (HA) at
Charing Cross with a
diverted Edinburgh to
Glasgow Queen Street
Low Level service.
Taken in June 2016.

No. 158733 (HA) arrives at Greenfaulds station with the 11:12 Falkirk Grahamston to Glasgow Queen Street service. Taken in May 2014.

No. 170456 (HA) leading a six-car service arrives at Falkirk High with the 09:45 Edinburgh to Glasgow Queen Street service. Taken in December 2017.

Six-car 156, unit 499 (CK) leading, at Cardross with the 12:42 Glasgow Queen Street to Oban and Mallaig service. Taken in May 2018.

No. 150284 (HA) arrives at platform 16 Edinburgh with a local service from Kirkcaldy. Note the parcels traffic still being handled. Taken in July 1988.

Four-car 158, unit 782 (HA) trailing, at Edinburgh Gateway station with the 07:06 Perth to Edinburgh service. This station was opened in December 2016 for connections to the airport. Taken in August 2018.

No. 140001 (HQ) at Glasgow Central platform 4. This was the forerunner to the modern-day pacers and sprinters. It was being tested out on various lines on the south side of Glasgow. On this occasion it was about to depart with a service to East Kilbride. Taken in August 1981.

Five-car 221 at Shilford Summit between Lugton and Barrhead with the 09:00 Carlisle to Glasgow Central diverted Virgin service. Taken in February 2016.

No. 158749 (NH) arrives at Haymarket with an Edinburgh to Manchester Airport service. Taken in June 2001.

Two sets of Class 141 units lie in Barclays Yard Kilmarnock awaiting repairs. Note on the far left a withdrawn 303, which had been shunted into the yard awaiting onward movement to the scrap man. Taken in August 1989.

Six-car 158, unit 745 (HA) leading, approaches Falkirk High with the 08:00 Glasgow Queen Street to Edinburgh service. Taken in September 1999.

No. 150257 (HA) at Edinburgh Waverley with a service to Cardenden. Taken in August 1991.

No. 158741 (HA) at Inverness. This unit had arrived with a service from Aberdeen. Taken in May 1992.

No. 158732 (HA) approaches Aberdeen with a service from Edinburgh. Taken in May 1992.

No. 156446 (IS) at Aberdeen with a service to Inverness. This unit was later transferred to Corkerhill in September 2000. Taken in May 1992.

No. 156505 (CK) in Strathclyde orange at Stranraer Harbour having arrived with the 08:13 service from Glasgow Central. Taken in May 1992.

No. 156453 (CK) at Crianlarich with a service from Mallaig. The unit is about to couple up onto the rear of the Oban portion. Both units would then go forward to Glasgow Queen Street. Taken in May 1992.

No. 158703 (HA) at Glasgow Queen Street with the 11:40 service to Aberdeen. Taken in March 1993.

No. 142004 (NH) in the sidings at Barclays Works Kilmarnock. The unit was up for minor repairs. Note the large building in the background under construction. This is now owned by Wabtec and continues to carry out railway vehicle repairs. Taken in February 1991.

No. 156424 (NH) passes Annan signalbox with the Sunday 14:33 Dumfries to Carlisle service. Taken in April 1993.

Five-car 221 passes New Cumnock signalbox with the 08:00 diverted Virgin service from Glasgow Central to Carlisle. Taken in January 2016.

No. 156434 (CK) at Glasgow Central with the 11:07 service to Barrhead. Taken in October 2003.

No. 158728 (HA) fifty-seven coach at Barclays Kilmarnock. The other half was inside the shed. The unit was getting an interior refurbishment. Taken in February 1997.

No. 150284 (HA) at Glasgow Central having just arrived with a service from Edinburgh Waverley via Shotts. Normally these services at this time were in the hands of Class 156s but due to a failure, No. 150284 was utilised instead. Taken in July 1997.

No. 156437 (CK) passes Westerton station with a Milngavie to Glasgow Queen Street service. Diesels were in use due to the overhead power being shut down for repairs. Taken in July 1998.

Four-car 158/156 combination, with 724 (HA) leading, arrives at Edinburgh with a service from Dunblane. Taken in May 1992.

No. 158728 (HA) at Shotts with the 13:06 Edinburgh to Glasgow Central service. Taken in November 2009.

No. 156508 (CK) departs from Kirkconnel with the 17:36 Newcastle to Stranraer Harbour service. Taken in April 1995.

Four-car 158, unit 719 (HA) leading, arrives at Perth with the 07:10 Glasgow Queen Street to Inverness service. Taken in July 1993.

Above left: No. 156432 (CK) on the Giffen branch near Barrmill with a test train. The test was in connection with the emergency services who carried out an exercise the following day. Taken in July 2001.

Above right: Four-car 156, unit 509 (CK) leading, with a Branch Line Society railtour near Mossblown on the single line between Annbank Junction and Newton-on-Ayr. Taken in August 1992.

No. 150262 (HA) departs Glasgow Queen Street with a local service for Cumbernauld. Taken in September 2000.

No. 170406 (HA) at Haymarket with the 08:30 Edinburgh Waverley to Glasgow Queen Street service. Note the snow bag over the coupler to protect against the elements. Taken in March 2001.

No. 158711 (ISD) at Cowdenbeath having just arrived with a local service from Edinburgh. Taken in March 2001.

No. 153367 (HT) at Carlisle having just arrived with a local service from Barrow. These units worked between Carlisle and Dumfries during the early 1990s. Taken in May 1992.

No. 170401 (HA) at Aberdeen. This unit had worked the 07:42 service from Glasgow Queen Street. Taken in June 2001.

Four-car 156 unit 500 (CK), in its home shed of Corkerhill depot, receiving repairs from the maintenance staff. Taken in January 2018.

No. 170472 (HA) passes Alexandria Parade with a diverted Glasgow Queen Street Low Level to Edinburgh service. Taken in June 2016.

Six-car 158, unit 722 (HA) leading, approaches Haymarket station with ECS from the nearby depot to Edinburgh Waverley. Taken in March 2001.

No. 140001 (HQ) seen at Eglinton Street outside Glasgow Central. The unit was on test on a local service from Barrhead. This grab shot taken from unit 311107 (GW). Taken in August 1981.

No. 170401 (HA)
and No. 158728 (HA)
at Aberdeen. The
170 had just arrived
with a service from
Edinburgh and the
158 is about to depart
with an Inverness
working. Taken in
June 2001.

No. 158749 (NH)
near Lamington
with a Manchester
Airport to Edinburgh
service. Taken in
November 2001.

Four-car 158, unit
727 (HA) trailing,
at Tweedbank
with a service from
Edinburgh. Will
this service ever be
extended to Carlisle?
Taken October 2015.